D1554739

Praise for:

The Way of Martial Arts for Kids . . .

"This book doesn't just help kids, it helps parents know what to expect and help their kids succeed."

– Lawrence Kane

Author of *Martial Arts Instruction: Applying Educational Theory and Communication Techniques in the Dojo*

"I wish I had this book when I was a kid. Often you can hear your instructor say things and it doesn't stick. Having it in writing makes a big difference."

– Robert Wittauer

Owner and Instructor, Emerald City Judo

The Way of Martial Arts for Kids

Getting the Most Out of Your Training

By Kris Wilder

Copyright © 2008 by Kris Wilder

ISBN 0-7414-4489-5

Published by:

PUBLISHING.COM

1094 New DeHaven Street, Suite 100
West Conshohocken, PA 19428-2713
Info@buybooksontheweb.com
www.buybooksontheweb.com
Toll-free (877) BUY BOOK
Local Phone (610) 941-9999
Fax (610) 941-9959

Printed in the United States of America
Printed on Recycled Paper
Published April 2008

Table of Contents

Dedication

To all of the kids that diligently come to the *dojo*, work hard and have a great time. Your successes and failures, both big and small, are the reasons that parents have hope for the future, smiles on their faces, and a deep joy that only a parent or teacher can know.

Foreword for Kids

Black belt! Being a black belt sounds really cool. It is impressive because it comes from hard work, sticking with your goals even when they are tough to achieve, and learning skills that most people don't have. If someone says you're a black belt it means all of those things and more in one symbol, one belt.

Martial arts are awesome. You can learn real-life fighting skills like kicking, punching, throwing, or grappling. Maybe you want to pick up a weapon too, learn how to use a sword or a staff or a set of *nunchaku* sticks like you see in the movies. You can do that too.

But it all comes at a price. Sure, your parents have to pay your instructor to teach you, but that's not what I'm talking about here. Learning real martial arts takes a lot of responsibility. You need to earn the right to learn fighting skills or practice with weapons. You need to earn those belt ranks.

First off, you have to convince your parents that you're really committed to learning the art. Classes are expensive. Uniforms, practice weapons, safety pads, advancement fees and things like that can really add up over time. They love you and want you to have fun and be the best you can be. It's only fair for you to hold up your end of the bargain. You need to be committed because your parents are. And you've also got to demonstrate the same thing to your instructors.

You must show up to class on time, pay attention, and work hard. You will probably even have to practice a little outside of the training hall too, yet you also have to get your schoolwork done and finish all your chores first. That means being smart with your time.

To begin with, you will get in great physical shape, earn new ranks, and pick up some really cool skills. You will earn belts or patches and certificates to hang on your wall that show the world all that you have done. With these accomplishments you will feel great about yourself and what you can do. And, you will almost certainly make a bunch of great new friends. The training hall isn't just a classroom, it's a community too.

You will not only learn how to fight for real, but you will also come to understand when you should or shouldn't do it. You will learn to use your smarts and find ways to deal with bullies that don't mean fighting or getting in trouble. And, if you try real hard, you will even earn some medals and trophies along the way too. It's very rewarding and fun stuff.

Take the advice you read in this book to heart and you will succeed in ways you've only dreamed of. Remember that everybody works hard, everybody starts at the beginning, and nothing is for free.

Foreword for Parents

At younger ages and ranks the training hall looks much like a noisy, rambunctious daycare, but it's not. It's a *dojang*, a *dojo*, or *kwoon*, a place to learn the martial way. This atmosphere is both challenging and very rewarding for the instructors.

Among the hordes of kids in class, a few stand out notably from the crowd. These are the ones who are a pleasure to teach, the ones who can earn special time, attention, and opportunities that are simply not available for everyone.

These kids excel because their parents have made a special effort to learn a little of how a martial arts school works, the unique brand of Asian organization and discipline that comes from the martial arts. Maybe it's an invitation to a tournament or a place on a demonstration team. Maybe it's a chance for leadership, to help teach others in class. Perhaps it's a special seminar that's only offered to the best students.

The book you hold in your hands is unique. It is about how your child can become one of those few exemplary learners who excel in the training hall as well as in life. The advice herein is straightforward, easy to understand, and written with a child-reader in mind. Wilder *Sensei* is a phenomenal instructor with years of experience. He has coached kids through the ranks from raw newcomers to experienced black belts. His students have gone on to become world-class scholars and business leaders.

I suggest that you purchase this book not only for your child but also for yourself. Armed with the knowledge it contains you can help ensure that your child will succeed. After all, learning begins at home. While the martial arts instructor knows his art, you know your child. Together you can help him or her achieve darn near anything.

Lawrence A. Kane

Author of *Martial Arts Instruction*; co-author of *The Way to Black Belt*

Acknowledgments

To James Harrell V, Audrey Vann, Gregory Vassiliou, Christopher Riley Izaya Wylde-Page, Dori Wylde-Page, Christopher Nunez, Shean Juta, Kacy Starr, Lindsay Vanderpool, Felix Bosques, Joseph Lamp, and Leanne Starr for lending their smiling faces to this book. Thanks a million.

And a special thank you to Laura Vanderpool for bringing her special brand of insight and thoughtful comments to this project.

Introduction

The martial arts are fun, but they are also hard work. Nothing in life that is worth having, or of value, comes easily. You must work for it. You need to set your mind that you are going to do something, pick a target and start working toward that target. Even the littlest steps in the right direction are progress. Sometimes you will make great leaps, other times you will take little steps. If you are set on your path, heading for your goal, your every step, no matter how big or how small, is still moving toward that goal.

This book can help you make the work easier and also make it more fun. In this book you will find little ideas that will make a big difference for you. So, as you read this book, think about all the ideas and how to make them work for you.

How to Use This Book

First, there is no right or wrong way to use this book. It is not like homework that has to be done by tomorrow. You can go as fast or as slow as you want and read it in any order you want too; it is totally up to you. Here are a few ideas of ways to use this book that you might like. Like I said, this is all about you and how you want to do it:

- Read the whole book as you please; relax and enjoy it: don't hurry. After you have read it, leave it next to your bed, or put it in your back pack and just read a few pages when you want to refresh your memory.

- Read the whole book and then go back and read one chapter and do what that chapter says until you have it. That could be a day, a week, or a month, whatever it takes because you control the speed. Some chapters have action items, things for you to try out; look for those items and see how you can use them in your training and daily life.

- If some of the ideas are hard to understand, talk with your parents and have them explain what it means. Moms and Dads are always happy to help you get better and succeed.

- Write in your book! Yes, it is yours and it is about learning so if you want you can highlight parts you like, or write in it with a pen or pencil, draw pictures, whatever helps you remember and learn.

Your School is a Special Place

A friend of mine used to leave trash wherever it lay in his apartment. He once walked past a pop can on the floor of his apartment for three weeks before his roommate finally picked it up! You know what? His karate uniform was dirty too. He didn't take care of the place where he lived, he didn't take care of his karate uniform and you can sure bet he didn't take care of the *dojo* either. In fact, he would often watch others clean and prepare the floor for training. He simply didn't take pride in his own life and it carried over to the *dojo*.

It doesn't make any difference if your martial arts school is called a *dojo*, a *kwoon*, or a studio, it is all the same. It is a special place that needs to be treated that way. If you go to church, synagogue, temple, or some other place of worship you try to be on your best behavior. A martial arts school is not like religion or a church, but it does require you to act your best. This means showing respect to your instructor and to the other students, being a good listener and following directions well. It also means following the rules of the *dojo*, such as bowing before you walk on to the *dojo* floor or putting your shoes in a certain place, and it means thinking of your school's reputation when you're out in public because you want your behavior to reflect well on the *dojo*. When you act your best you learn better and people also treat you better. So best behavior! Always be on your best behavior.

Your Parents

I was pretty lucky that my parents explained to me at a pretty young age that they were my parents and they were going to do the best for me. Sometimes that meant that I didn't get to do what I wanted to do, but it also meant a lot of good things. My parents went out of their way to give me, and I do mean *give*, because I didn't earn it, a really good life as a kid. They took me to a World's Fair and taught me things that most kids don't learn how to do. I knew how to throw a pot (that means make a clay pottery bowl) on a potter's wheel, and use power tools at a young age. We rode motorcycles, hunted, and fished, and I was able to drive a truck on the farm by the time I was twelve. Other kids did different things because every parent has a different set of gifts that they offer to their children. In your case, you are pretty lucky to have parents that will let you take martial arts. It takes a lot of time, effort and money on the part of your parents for you to do what you do. You can't drive yourself, so they drive you; you probably can't even pay for the gas to put in the car or van. Your parents also make sure your uniform is clean and your school dues are paid on time. If you participate in tournaments or demonstrations, they take time off to attend them with you and make sure your permission slips are filled out properly. I mean, really, they could be doing something else, couldn't they? So the next time you feel like complaining or ducking out of class, remember that your parents have already set aside the time, paid the money, and made every effort to help you succeed. You owe them your best effort in return; it's only fair.

Your Instructor

When I was in grade school I got pretty good grades, and then something happened: I got a tough teacher. She wasn't really tough, but that was the way I saw it. The truth was she saw more in me than I saw in myself. That seemed odd to me because I was pretty sure I knew myself. The fact was she wouldn't let me get away with not doing my best work. It was hard, very hard, but she made me realize that I was better than I thought and in some ways not as good as I believed myself to be. My teacher had gone to school just like I had, then went to college, and then had been teaching for more years that I had been going to school.

Your martial arts instructor has quite possibly been training in the martial arts longer than you have been alive. That is a long time! When you get a chance, ask your martial arts instructor and you'll likely find this to be true. They know what they are doing and you should trust them when it comes to the martial arts. There are things they know about the martial arts that they won't even show you for years. You have to earn the right to be shown and taught things as you continue to train, when you show increasing responsibility as well as improvement in the techniques you have already been taught. Most instructors don't brag about such things, but trust me; they are showing you only a small part of all they know. So the next time you think you might want be a little smart to your instructor, or decide to not pay attention, remember they know a lot, and you are only a beginner.

Personal Hygiene

Hygiene is an unusual word. It means practices of cleanliness that are good for peoples' health. So personal hygiene is to make yourself clean so you will have good health and not get sick. Now, I have to tell you that as kid I never really had a sense of my own dirt. Sometimes my mother would not even let us in the house! She would just hand us a broom and make my brother and me beat each other until enough dirt was off of us to let us in the house. And then she only let us in on the way to the bath. Hygiene is really important for adults too. Think about it! Would you like it if the dentist put dirty fingers in your mouth, or have a doctor with lunch spilled on the front of their shirt work on you? I think not.

You need to be clean when you train in martial arts. You spend a lot of time grabbing, pushing, shoving, pulling, punching, well, you get the idea – there is a lot of contact with other students in the school. Your hands need to be clean; your uniform needs to be clean too. Also, check your toenails and fingernails to make sure they are clean and trimmed. A regular shower or bath goes a long way in keeping clean. Likewise, combing your hair and brushing your teeth help you look good and smell good. At the school, when you use the restroom, don't forget to wash your hands with soap and warm water. And while we're on the subject, remember to flush the toilet. Your fellow students will be glad you did!

Your Uniform

Have you noticed that every sports team has a uniform? Your soccer team has its colors; your favorite football team has its mascot, like a cougar, or an eagle. These uniforms, colors and mascots separate you from the other team so you know who is on your team or who to cheer for. In the martial arts the uniform does the same thing.

Every martial arts school has a uniform. Some are specially made uniforms like a *dogi* (a karate uniform) or a *dobak* (a Taekwondo uniform); some schools use different colored uniforms, or all white or all black; some a t-shirt and sweat pants. And you know what? It doesn't make any difference! Whatever your school wears is the right uniform to wear. What *does* make a difference is that you treat your uniform well. When you're not wearing it you should hang it up in a closet or fold it nicely and put it in a dresser drawer. Tossing your uniform on the floor of the van on the way to soccer is no way to treat it. The same goes for the floor of your room or home. The floor of any room is not a place for your uniform. Keep your uniform clean too. A dirty, smelly uniform might be funny to you but not to your instructor. If you have to eat in your uniform on the way the class (hey, it happens sometimes) be extra careful not to spill on it, (and don't forget to wipe your face too). A clean and well-cared for uniform, when worn, shows pride and respect for the art you are practicing and for your school as well. Plus, it looks cooler.

Your Belt

I knew a guy who had been in the United States Marines; he had been in combat and had been a drill instructor too. One time he took me into his home office and library and on his wall, framed, was a display of medals. These medals had ribbons and designs on them. I went through some of them and asked what this one was for and that one. The medals ranged from "marksmanship" (that is really good shooting with a rifle), and serving in Vietnam in the 1960s. It was impressive. Now, as impressive as all those medals are it would be really weird to see him go to the local store with them all pinned on his shirt. In fact, we would think he was some kind of nut!

Most martial arts schools use belts to show how far you have progressed. It is a lot like the uniform, and medals we just talked about. Whatever you school does is fine. In fact, a lot of kids like to talk to other kids from other martial arts schools and compare the different belt ranks. You would be amazed at the differences! In some schools a blue belt is higher than a green belt, in others it is the opposite – green is higher than blue. And you know what? Some schools don't even use a blue belt! It can get kind of crazy. The important thing is that you know what it's worth and how hard you worked to get it. That means it should be treated with respect! Same as with your uniform, don't just throw your belt on a bench when you are done training...hang it up or fold it with your uniform. The great thing is; when you hang up your belt or fold it together with your uniform you will always know where it is!

Fighting

One time this friend of mine got in a fight and the police came to break it up. After they broke it up they separated the two fighters and asked a few questions. After that was over, they decided to arrest my friend and take him to jail. My friend then asked the police, "Hey, didn't the other person I was fighting with say they started it and hit me first?" One police officer said, "Yes, you are right," and turned and arrested the other person too. Both of the people that got into the fight wound up in jail that night. Nobody won; nobody went home the victor that night.

Today you are told never to get into a fight. It just means big trouble, especially when you're at school, because you will be suspended or expelled. Truth is, fighting is really never a good idea and it is not a way to fix things. People just get hurt. And remember; even if you didn't start the fight you will still get in the most trouble because you take martial arts. So you better think real hard before deciding to fight. You may win the fight but you will lose a lot more – your reputation, privileges, maybe some friends as well. Choosing not to fight is really the choice that takes the most courage. And it is the right one to make. In a fight, everybody loses.

Sparring

Some twenty years ago I had my knee dislocated while sparring. Back then we didn't use pads, gloves, or head gear. Was I mad or upset when it happened? No! I was in pain! The important part was that the guy I was sparring didn't mean to dislocate my knee; he was not being extra aggressive and he didn't mean to hurt me. In fact, we used to get together outside of class regularly to work on our martial arts. I tell you this story because, frankly, it just is not going to happen to you. The way things are today, you are protected and safe. You don't really need to worry about getting hurt.

Sparring can be a lot of fun. It can also be scary sometimes, especially when you get matched up with another kid that has a higher rank or is bigger than you. But you have protective pads on and your instructor is there to make sure no one gets hurt. So the only thing that might get hurt is your feelings. It is OK to be worried about your feelings, but in this case all you need to do is relax, take a deep breath and have some fun. A funny thing happens when you have fun, so does everybody else! And they will join in with you because everybody likes a fun person. So the next time you spar, remember: the more you relax the more fun it will be!

Questions

"If Godzilla came around the corner right now, what would you do?" This is the kind of question my cousin Monte was fond of asking while we rode in the back of the car. Even as a kid I thought those were really dumb questions! I mean, come on! Godzilla is not real and we are driving down the road; there is no corner! Good grief.

It's OK to ask questions sometimes. If you ask good questions and really listen to the answers, you can learn a lot. And, if others ask questions, you should pay attention to those answers too. But there are good questions and not-so-good questions. In class, asking a question that starts with "What if..." is not good. A "what if" question is about something that *might* happen, not about what is happening right now. Stop before you ask the question and insert the word "when" instead of "what" – it almost always makes a better question. Here is an example: "When I put my arm like this to block, it doesn't seem to work." This asks about something you're doing in class right now that you have a question about. If you ask a question this way, the instructor and the students know exactly what you're talking about and the answer you get will make more sense. Remember: use the word "when" instead of "what" and make sure the question is about what is happening right now.

Forms

People use lots of different ways to tell a story. In Europe during the Middle Ages before cell phones, newspapers and the Internet, they had troubadours. These people would go from town to town entertaining the local people with stories that they had made into songs. Another example from long ago is the Town Crier. Now that was a real job! The Town Crier would yell out the news of the day so the town knew what was going on. Remember, this was at time before television or radio, so this was the main way people got important information. In prehistoric times, people told stories in paintings, on paper, walls of caves, or even animal skins.

Forms or kata (the Japanese word for form) are pretty important things when it comes to the martial arts. It might not seem like it but it is true. Kata are filled with an amazing amount of information and ideas. Think of it this way. If a person that lived a long way away wanted to tell you a story they might send you a book of the story. Then you could read it, enjoy the story and maybe share it with someone else too. A form or kata is the same way. Created hundreds of years ago, forms were passed on from teacher to student, like a story told not in words but in moves! Each form is a story told from a person from a long time ago about best ways to fight. Each is kind of a book that you can read over and over again and learn important things from every time. So make sure you learn your forms well because some day you might be asked to share the form with someone else and you want to get the story right!

Who's Responsible? You!

"Showing up for work on time is the easiest thing you are going to do all day," is what my old business partner used to say to the people that worked for us, and he was right. To people that had a problem with being late, he would add, "How about I just pay you when I feel like it?" What he was saying was that people depend on each other and that being on time is important for you and for others. Being on time means that you think that what is going to happen is important, whether it is at work (or in your case, school) or martial arts class.

It is important to get to class on time. Your parents help you get to class – besides paying for your classes, they probably feed you ahead of time and drive you to or from the school. Your job is to be responsible for your uniform and belt as well as your shoes and sometimes also your coat. One of the most annoying things for a parent to hear when you're running out the door is "I can't find my belt" or uniform, shoes, or water bottle. A good way to keep this from happening is to always put your uniform in the same place so you don't have to look for it. Also, a good tip is to start getting ready to leave for class a couple of minutes early so you're not rushed and forget things. Challenge yourself to see if you can go a day without saying, "I can't find."

Get to Class Early

By getting to class early, oftentimes you can get a little bit of special instruction or see another class practicing. Both are good things, but the most important part of getting to class early is that you are ready to train when class begins. Once in awhile you just can't help being late, but doing it all the time tells the instructor that you are not serious about your training. It is also disrespectful to your instructor and the other students. Think about it this way. If you are late all the time you might as well walk up to the instructor and say right to their face, "Whatever I was doing was more important than this." Wow, would you do that? Well, if you are late every class you might as well be saying just that. So make every effort to be early to class. Being early tells everybody, "Hey, this is important!"

Finally, it is better to be early than late to class. I used to be early in the hope that my instructor would show me something special, and you know what? He did. He showed me things and spent time with me because my actions showed him that I valued what he had to teach.

Do What You are Asked to Do

Imagine a world where everybody did exactly what *they* wanted to do all the time and ignored what people asked of each other. When you went to the store the people at the store would just make up a price. When if you bought a pack of gum they might charge you twenty dollars and then your friend who bought two packs of the same gum only a penny, just because the checker felt like it. Or imagine going to get an ice cream cone and getting a cone of raw hamburger instead? And, wouldn't it be really bad if you asked the ice cream person five times in a row for a scoop of ice cream and you got raw hamburger every time? That would be even more frustrating. You ask for an ice cream cone and that is what you expect. The way it really works, of course, is that the checker at the store charges you what their boss says to charge you, not what they think is a good idea. The person behind the counter that scoops your ice cream gives you the kind of ice cream you ask for.

How many times have you heard your parents say things like, "I have asked you a million times." Or, "Didn't you hear me?" Or something like that. That is not really a good thing, and it should never happen in the martial arts school. What would it be like if every kid in the class had to be told the same thing over and over all the time? You would get nothing done; that is all class time would be! That's why most of the time you *do* pay attention in martial arts class – you know how annoying it would be if people didn't, and probably also know your instructor wouldn't put up with it.

Well, try a little of that at home, too. The next time you hear your Mom or Dad ask you to do something, just say "OK," and do whatever it is they want you to do – put on your shoes, clean your room, take out the trash, whatever – don't make them ask you twice. Just like you would in your martial arts school.

If You are Older

When I was a kid there was this older student that I thought was just the coolest guy on the planet. He was a super athlete at our school; he was a punter for the football team (wow, he was a specialist) and he was a letterman, meaning he played varsity sports. Later on I would be a letterman too and play football, although I never was a punter. This older guy never even knew I was watching how he did stuff, but he was a role model for me. That means I looked up to him and tried to copy him.

If you are an older kid in class you have a job you might not know about. That job is to be a class leader. You may well be a role model for somebody like the football punter I copied. You don't get a special patch or ribbon but you get the job anyway. Don't you know an older kid that you think is pretty cool? They seem to have it all together and get to do things that you think are really fun. Well, guess what? There are younger kids in the martial arts school that are looking at you the same way! It is true! So if you are one of the older kids in class you have other kids looking at you to see what they are supposed to do and how they are supposed to act. This job you probably didn't know about means you need to act really good in class. This doesn't mean telling other kids what to do; that is the instructor's job. Your job is to do what the instructor asks the class to do and do it really well. You watch; soon the younger kids will be copying you.

If You are Younger

If you are one of the youngest kids in the class it can be hard. Everybody is bigger, stronger and seems to do things better. Don't worry about it. The instructor knows whether or not you are working hard and they know how hard it can be if you are the smallest or the youngest in class.

Here is a tip for you: look for the best student in class and copy them! Yes, copy them! You will get better faster and you will look really good too. Soon you will be helping out the next new kid to feel at home in your school. And while I am at it, let me add one other tip that will make the biggest difference: keep your eyes on the instructor. If you watch your instructor's every move you will get better faster, enjoy class, more and not get in trouble, all good things. So next class, choose one thing to do: copy a really good student or keep your eyes on the instructor.

Use the Mirrors the Right Way

A lot of martial arts schools have mirrors on the walls. These mirrors are so you can see what you're doing and make your form better. You can see yourself punch from the side if you want or you can look at somebody who is better than you and see how they do something. Mirrors are not for making faces in, or for pressing your hands and face on. If a mirror is dirty with fingerprints, somebody has to clean them (probably the instructor), and being silly in the mirror (which maybe will make others laugh and make you popular) is distracting to other students and disrespectful of the instructor. So, while you might be tempted, leave the funny faces at home and use the school mirrors for the right reason – to help you and the rest of the students improve.

Focus, Focus, Focus

Here are two tips you can use to help you get more out of the mirrors at your martial arts school:

-    Start small: Choose to look at only one thing; stances are a good place to start, and just look at that part of your body during your class time. Focus on making your stance look just like the way your instructor does it. How deep does your instructor bend their knee? Can you copy them?

-    Find the best student in the class and copy them – their moves, their stances, and their attitude. This means if they are standing straight, you stand straight; if they are running, you run; you get the picture. If you watch them through the mirror, the chances of them catching you copying them are very small and you will secretly get better.

Visiting the Advanced Class

Staying with my cousin one week when I was in high school, I went with him to his college classes. I never signed up; I never checked in or anything. He said, "Come with me to my classes; see what college is like," so I did and I liked it – a lot. I was seeing and hearing things that were really interesting. When I went back to my school I was able to see where my high school education was going; it helped me make sense of what I was learning. You might get the same benefit from visiting the advanced or senior class at your martial arts school.

First you need to ask your instructor if you can do it, but see if you can visit an advanced class or maybe an adult class just to watch. It is a great way to see what all those moves you're learning look like when more advanced students are doing them, and get a sneak peek into what you will be learning a little later on. Most of the time you are in a class with other kids that are pretty close to your own level. Sometimes just watching others that are at a higher level can really help you understand what you are trying to do. Think of it like skipping ahead in a book or a movie to see how it ends – and how knowing the ending changes the way you see the book, the movie, or in this case, the martial arts. Try it – it will make your martial arts better.

School Comes First

As a martial arts teacher sometimes students come to me and say, "Sorry I was not in class yesterday, I had too much homework." And I always say, "That's OK, school comes first," and it's true. School always comes first. Martial arts is something you can do all your life, but school goes away after a while. And you need to do the best you can while you're there. So if you need to do your school work and miss class once in awhile, do it and don't feel bad about it. Of course you'll want to try real hard to get your school work done so you don't miss too many classes, but school work is more important. I'll bet you didn't know that the Samurai, the old Japanese warriors, used to spend a lot of time learning how to write with ink and paint brushes and compose poetry! They were expected to learn a lot more than just how to fight. So see, no matter who you are, school is important!

Play Other Sports

As a kid you have the chance to do a lot of different sports and activities – you can dance, play baseball, football, or run track – they are all good things to do and might not be something you do when you're older. The chance to play on teams with your schoolmates and friends and to learn a lot of different sports is something you should not miss out on. Another point is you get to learn life lessons you usually don't get to learn someplace else. What does that mean? Life lessons? It means that you will have more experience, more things that have happened to you, and you can use those things to make good choices in your life.

Here is a little story that happened to me. In college I was training in karate and one evening we had a karate party celebrating a bunch of advancements by students. The food at the party was good and the people were happy. Later in the evening I had a moment to chat with the head instructor – he was then a very famous karate instructor and still is today for that matter. As we talked I told him I really admired his karate skill and that I hoped one day to be as good as him. He smiled and nodded a simple "Thank you." I went on and said that I wanted to train like him and then that would put me on the path to being like him. He paused a moment and said, "You don't want to be like me; all I can do is karate. You are in college you can do many more things than I can." I was really hit hard by that comment. The instructor's words were so honest and real that I remember what he said today some twenty-five years later.

What that karate master was saying is you need to do other things; don't live a small life. What I am saying is that same thing except when you have a chance to play sports you should do it and then come back to the martial arts. Enjoy the baseball, the drum lessons, or the Pop Warner football. The martial arts are always going to be around for your whole life.

No Food Allowed

Walking up the steps to the *dojo* one afternoon I ran into one of my friends sitting on the steps eating a sandwich. I asked him, "What are you doing eating on the steps like this?" He said, "I missed lunch and I need to eat something before class or I am going to just pass out." He then went on to say, "And anyway you don't take food into the *dojo*." Then he took a couple of the biggest bites of sandwich I had ever seen in an effort to get it eaten before training began.

Eating in the martial arts studio is not a good idea. The studio is for martial arts; it is not a restaurant. So if you need to finish eating because you had a really busy day, eat in the car, or outside of the school; don't bring it into the school. There should never be a chance of getting food on the floor of the school. The floor needs to be clean at all times, for safety and because people sit on it sometimes and don't want their uniforms to get dirty. Besides, you don't want to risk spilling on your uniform, and no one wants to smell your burrito in class either. So don't bring your food into the martial arts school. It really is that simple.

Water

Water is really important. When you get thirsty your body is telling you it needs water. When your body gets thirsty it is not asking for a can of soda pop or a fruit juice, it needs good water and that is what you should give it. Water doesn't have sugar or coloring added to it. If your body needed those things I guess the lakes and rivers would be made of grape soda pop! So follow nature's lead and drink water when you are thirsty from training in martial arts. Your body will thank you for it. Soda pop has too much sugar in it (really it is high fructose corn syrup) and fruit juices have a different kind of sugar in it, but the bottom line is too much sugar is bad for your body. And if you think diet soda pop is better, read this: Carbonated water, caramel color, aspartame, phosphoric acid, polycarbon bionate, potassium citrate, potassium benzoate, caffeine, phenylalanine.

Now for the test. Think you know what all those things are? Of course not, in fact one of the words is completely made up; it is not real! And you can't tell the difference. Do you really want to put that in your body? No! Drink water; it is the safest bet.

Pay Attention or Miss Out

Just like in your regular school, if you don't pay attention in class you are going to miss out. It might not seem like a big deal but the "miss outs" when you are not listening begin to add up.

A good attitude makes all the difference!

One minute of making faces in the mirror adds up to eight minutes a month. Multiply that for all twelve months of a year and you will have wasted ninety-six minutes, over an hour and a half. Miss-outs add up. I have one student that has to go to the restroom every class. Now let's add up the training time he has missed. He has been training two years. Multiply the three minutes for each restroom break by two classes a week, then by fifty weeks of classes. Figure it out; you will be amazed.

Bullies

Bullies are kids that don't think too much of themselves. That is why they bully – it is a fast way for a bully to feel better about whom they are. Bullies are looking for kids that are easy to push around. Did you ever see a bully take on the biggest kid in school? Not very often! The most important thing you can do with a bully is let them know that you are not going to be bullied. Here are a few tips. Stay around friends: Bullies don't like groups very much. Keep your distance: Bullies like to push and if you are not close enough they can't push you. And finally, if you can just walk to a teacher or the school office without saying anything, that's good too: Once the bully figures out where you are going they will stop following you. These are just some of the tricks you can use. Truth is, a lot of bullies just feel really bad about themselves and take their bad feelings out on other people. Here is something to try, when the bully is not actually bullying you, come up to them and invite them to a party, or invite them to play with you and your friends. I'll bet if you put your mind to it you can think up a couple of ideas too on how to handle a bully all by yourself.

Wearing Your Math Test Around Your Waist

When you take a test at school and you do well, you usually just get a mark on your paper. Oh sure, it is important and it adds up over time but when you do well in a martial arts test you actually wear the grade around your waist! And for a long time! So pay attention, work hard, and be ready for your next test because how well you do will not just be a mark on a piece of paper, that grade is going to be wrapped around your waist for everybody to see.

School Brothers and Sisters

The other kids at the martial arts school are not really your brothers and sisters, but it might be useful to think of them that way. What happens when you are training in martial arts is different than in other kinds of classes. You are learning an art form that if you are not careful you can hurt somebody. If you make a mistake in art class, nobody gets hurt; if you make a mistake in baseball you get charged with an error or you get put out. If you make a mistake in martial arts class, like not paying attention and doing the wrong move, somebody could get a black eye or bloody lip! So be respectful of the other kids you train with in the school. They trust you and you trust them, kind of like a brother or sister.

Ask a Senior Student for Help

A great way to get better is to ask somebody who has a higher rank to work with you. When you ask a higher-ranked student to work with you on a form or a technique, you will find that they don't say "no" too much. In fact, they'll probably be flattered you asked and will give you their best. This is a great way to get better fast. When you work with somebody that has a higher rank you have to work up to their belt rank and you get better. Do this next time you go to class, just ask for just one minute of help. You can say something like, "I need help with this technique; would you help me?" Try it. You will find it works and you get better.

Be Neat

Being neat is a big deal. Having a clean uniform is important because it tells everybody you take your training seriously. But it doesn't stop there. Having combed hair is important too. Check your hair to see if it is messy. If you have long hair, pull it back into a ponytail. If you have just eaten, check your face to make sure you don't have any food on your cheeks. Also you need to have clean finger and toe nails. Nobody wants to work with somebody who is dirty and being neat and clean tells everybody you are ready to learn.

Ask for Help

If you are having a problem understanding something that is being taught in classes ask for help. A lot of kids are kind of embarrassed to ask because they are afraid they might look stupid to the other kids or they are just shy. But you are supposed to ask good questions, at the right time of course. Every instructor wants you to be good and to get good you need to know what you are doing. So the next time you feel embarrassed to ask a question, relax and ask it anyway. And if anybody makes fun of you for asking a question for "not getting it," you just say, "I want to get better; what's wrong with that?"

Tournaments

Tournaments can be a lot of fun. Having all your friends from the school get together to go to a special event is pretty cool. It's exciting and a little scary at the same time. You will get butterflies in your stomach when it is your turn to do something. You might win, you might lose, and the same goes for your friends. One of the most important things to remember is, whatever you do, however you act, is going to be judged by others. That means you want to do your best, and, you want to act your best, even when you're not the one competing. You can lose a tournament and still win people's hearts by being a good sport and showing good manners. Everybody likes a well-mannered and nice person.

Another thing to remember is that people are going to look at you, look at your patch or figure out what school you are with, and then they are going to judge your instructor. And you would feel bad if you let your instructor and your school down with poor sportsmanship or rude behavior. This is a lot to remember, but I'll teach you a trick. Be on your best behavior all day and everything will be great. Then, when others judge you and your instructor, both will be judged well!

Being Sick

Being sick is part of being a kid. You know what it is like; one kid gets sick in school and pretty soon most of the kids have the same sickness too. The question is, should you come to the martial arts school and train even if you are feeling a little bad? Here is how you decide. If you are getting sick, stay home; there is no need to give the cold or flu to others and you will do poorly in class. If you are not actually sick but just a little tired or feeling a little down, you go to class. Just like with school – if you're really sick it's important to stay home and not spread the germs around, but if you're just a little tired you still get up and go to school. With the martial arts it is just the same.

Your First Choice is Usually the Right Choice

You've probably had this happen. You're taking a multiple-choice test and get stuck on a problem that you know you've learned the answer to but can't remember. Same with your martial arts class – you're doing a form and you suddenly forget the next move. It happens. But here is a trick to get you back on track: go with your first choice! Really, it is that easy. Just think back quickly to what you first wanted to do before you froze and then do it. Soon you will get really good at this and begin to trust your own mind. Give it a try the next time you can't remember what to do and choose what your mind wanted you to do first. You're probably going to be right.

Be Helpful in the *Dojo*

Helping other students is the best thing you can do. Besides making them better, you will also notice that the more helpful you are the more you learn! The way this happens is pretty cool. When you help others it means you have to use words to explain what you are doing. When you use words it makes you think. When you think your brain is working and that makes you better! There are a lot of other important ways to be helpful too. Sweeping the school floor, helping others get their belts tied right or even being nice and working with a younger kid before class starts is a great way to make others feel better about themselves and you will too.

When You Get Angry or Frustrated

My instructor used to say, "The angrier you get the stupider you get." Boy is that the truth! The angrier you get the less you are able to think, and the more likely you'll make bad decisions or do or say something you'll wish you hadn't. Frustration is just a different kind of angry so watch out for anger and frustration because they can make you real dumb real fast. Here is a trick to get rid of anger or frustration. Take a deep breath, let it out real quick and flick your fingers at the ground like you are trying to shake water off of them. It works; try it! Stand up straight, take a deep breath in through your nose, the deepest breath you can make, and breathe out through your mouth. Then with your wrists really loose, flick your fingers at the ground. Do the "deep breath, blowing out, finger flick" two more times, then check how you feel. You will notice the difference!

Measure Yourself By Yourself Not Against Others

There is always going to be somebody better, faster, or stronger than you. However, there is only one of you and you are special. You are the only measuring stick that you should use to measure your actions and accomplishments. There is nothing wrong with looking at others and using them to inspire you to be your best, but trying to copy them to *become* them never works. A way of measuring yourself is to pick one thing, maybe a front kick, and work on it for a week then look back and ask yourself, "Am I better than I was before?" Now you have set a goal and measured yourself against yourself...and gotten better.

You are Smart

You know what? You are pretty smart. How can I say that without having met you? Easy; you are reading this book. If you are reading this book that means you are trying to get better at martial arts and that is a smart thing to do. You know that getting better at martial arts makes you better at other things in your life and that is important. Use your smarts every day, learn as much as you can and you will get smarter because the brain is just like a muscle - the more you use it the smarter you will get.

The Race is Not Always to the Swiftest

In every class there are kids that are really good and they don't seem to have to work too hard at it. And there are other students that have to work a little harder than the others to get what is being taught. One of the most important things you need to remember is an old saying, "The race is not always won by the fastest person." Often just working on your technique, showing up to class whenever there is class and doing what you are asked to do will make you better. It is just like growing up. You keep getting bigger but you don't notice it from day to day. Then suddenly you can't fit into your old pants and you realize, "Wow! I've grown a couple of inches!" Martial arts are the same way. I'll bet if you think about it there are a few things you do now that you couldn't do, or do much better than you could just three months ago. A little bit of hard work every day makes all the difference over time.

Push On Through the Tough Times

There is an old saying that goes like this, "Quitters never win and winners never quit." And it's true. What it really means is that in everything you do, and I mean everything, you are going to hit a few hard spots. Take a minute and think about cleaning your room. It's a big mess, you don't know where to start, and you get frustrated and want to give up. But then you just choose one thing, like putting away all your books, and do that. And then picking up clothes on the floor, or toys, one little job at a time. Eventually what was a big mess is nice and tidy. Or, maybe you have had to ride your bike up a hill and you got tired but you kept going. Maybe the hill you were trying to ride up was so steep you had to get off the bike and push it, but you didn't quit when it got tough. Martial arts is the same as pushing the bike up the hill. It can get tough but the view from the top of the hill is really good. Plus you get to ride the bike back down the hill. So the next time your martial arts class gets kind of tough you just need to stay with it; you will get to the top of the hill and it will be fun once you get there.

You Earned That Belt

Listen to your friends talk about their grades at school. When they do well they will say, "I got an A!" But when they get a bad grade, they will say, "The teacher gave me a bad grade." But that's not really that way it is in school or the martial arts studio. In school, it's you earning the good or the bad grades. In your martial arts class you are the one responsible for whether you do well or not. You either earn a rank or fail a test.

Girls and Boys, No Difference

In a martial arts school there is no difference between boys and girls. Everybody is expected to work hard, pay attention and do what they are supposed to do. Everybody wears the same kind of uniform and lines up according to rank. When you are a girl working with a boy or a boy working with a girl it makes no difference. Be strong, move swiftly and be confident in your skills. The instructor has the same expectations for both; that is to say, the instructor is sure that boys are just as good as girls when it comes to the martial arts.

Take Responsibility

When you forget you belt, whose belt is it? When your belt is not tied right, who tied it? When you're not paying attention, who doesn't hear the instructions? When you can't find your uniform, whose uniform is it? The answer is YOU and YOURS; they are all your responsibility. You forgot your belt, not your Mom or Dad; you tied your belt poorly; you weren't paying attention; and you couldn't find your uniform. One of the most important things a martial artist can do is take responsibility for their own things. An interesting thing is, when you take responsibility then you can take credit when you do something right, too. And doesn't that make you feel good? To be a good martial artist you have to own both the good and the bad.

There is More Beyond the Black Belt

A black belt is a very big deal and is a great goal to have, but remember that there is more after black belt – a lot more. The really good martial artist keeps on working once they get their black belt; in fact, they continue to learn for their entire life!

A black belt is like leaving high school; now you get to go to college and learn even more. There are more forms and more techniques after black belt and one real important thing to remember is you can always get better at what you already know. It is like when you started to learn how to read. First it was hard and you weren't very good, but you got better. Now if you go back and look at the things you used to have a hard time reading you laugh at how easy it is. Martial arts are a lot like that.

Don't Worry

My Grandmother said it really well; "Don't go borrowing trouble." What she meant was you don't need to make up in your head all the things that could go wrong. Have you ever done that? Those kinds of ideas start with the words, "What if..." Try it out for yourself. Pretend you have a martial arts test coming up real soon. Let's borrow some trouble now: "What if I freeze up and forget everything?" "What if my pants fall off?" "What if my belt explodes or catches on fire?" "What if my tongue grows too long and I trip over it?" Pretty silly ideas, huh? That is what borrowing trouble sounds like; just as silly as tripping over your tongue. So the next time you face a worry, see if you are using the words, "What if..." If you are, you are probably borrowing trouble.

A Test is a Chance to Show Off

My karate instructor once asked me why I did so badly in tests. I told him I was nervous and wanted to do well. He said, "Don't worry, all the people in the *dojo* are your friends." He went on to say, "A test is just a chance for you to show off to your friends." As soon as I looked at testing like that I never had a problem again.

If Your Friend Quits

Don't let your friends decide for you what you want to do. A lot of times if a friend quits martial arts, you will quit, but why? Are you quitting because your friend did? Or are you quitting because you really want to quit? And if you do quit, you should do something else. Just quitting so you can play more video games or watch more TV is not a good reason. Do you drink root beer because your friend drinks root beer, or do you drink root beer because you like it? If your friend decides they like to drink sour tomato juice instead of root beer is that a good reason to switch? No, if you like what you are doing then you should make up your own mind and not let your friend decide for you. And besides, they will still be your friend anyway.

If You Don't Get it, Break it Down

Here is a trick to help you get a new thing you are learning: break it down. What does "break it down" mean? It means instead of doing the whole thing you are trying to learn all at once, start with the very first part of it and get that part right. Like if you are learning a new kick, ask your instructor to show the very beginning to you. You might ask your instructor something like, "Excuse me, but does my foot start like this, or like this?" You will find that many times getting started the right way makes a huge difference and you will find it really easy to get the kick to work for you. Then, if you find there's another part that you don't understand you can work on that separately too before putting it all together. You can use this "break it down" way of figuring things out for just about anything. A good way of thinking about it is this: a brick wall, no matter how big it is, is built of little bricks stacked on top of one another.

Be Loud!

Being loud at a movie might get you in trouble; being loud in the classroom might get you in trouble too. There are lots of places we are supposed to be quiet and it makes sense. But in your martial arts school you are supposed to be loud! If you are asked a question, answer loudly! If you are punching a bag, yell loudly when you hit it! Not only is it fun, but it tells the instructor that you are having a good time and are paying attention to the lesson. In school be quiet; in the martial arts school be loud and proud!

After the Test – "I Need a Break."

It is really common for students to want to take a break after a test. They say, "Oh I worked hard, I deserve a break." And then they don't show up for the next class. After a test instructors often jump right into the new techniques you need to know for the next belt. Because of this you should take advantage of that class right after the test. The class will be smaller, you will get more time with the instructor and you will already be ahead of the other kids that decided to take a break.

Summertime

Summertime is a great time. It is warm, you don't have school, and you get to do other things you normally don't get to do. Sometimes kids think it's time for a break from martial arts class too. You think summertime is for relaxing or doing something else, maybe nothing at all, and you are wrong. Summertime is one of the best times to go to your martial arts school. With all those kids taking the summer off, that means they are out of your way and you get more attention. The instructor can help you more because the class is smaller. So show up during those summer months and get better faster.

Good Manners: "Please" and "Thank You"

Good manners go a long way. If you have good manners people will like you more; really, it works that way! In many martial arts schools the instructor is always called Mr. or Mrs., or Sensei. This is a sign of respect. If you add the words "please" and "thank you" to your talking you will do even better. And remember to use those manners outside of the martial arts school too; you will be surprised at how nicely people will treat you back.

Put Everything Where it Belongs

When you come to the martial arts school for class, everything belongs in a certain spot. Your shoes get put away so others don't trip over them and so everything is neat and tidy. Some schools have you line your shoes up on the edge of the floor with the fronts facing away from the floor; others have boxes on the wall. The point is everything gets put away. The benches or chairs are for sitting on, not for you to throw you coat or bag on and walk away. And there's a reason for that: a room where everything is in its place is easier to work in. It looks a lot nicer too. It is just like your parents say at home, "Pick it up!" "Put it away." It is no different at the martial arts school. Think about this: how many time have you said, "I can't find my shoes!" Well, whose shoes are they anyway? I would say that to my Dad, and he would say, "Well, the last time I wore them, I put them away." That is a silly thing to say because my shoes wouldn't fit his feet! But the point he was making was that those shoes are my responsibility, not his; in fact, they could never be his responsibility because he couldn't wear them if he wanted to. So put things where they belong. That way you will have order in your life and your life will be less stressful. The older you get the more things you have responsibility for, and you must be able to find your shoes, your homework, your books, your pants, your towel, and much more.

I Can't

The words "I can't" are words that mean "I give up." These are words you just should not use inside the martial arts school or anywhere else. Instead, try words like these: "I am working on it," "This is hard," or "I am having a difficult time." Here is a challenge: the next time you think of saying, "I can't," make up your own way of saying that you are not quitting and see how different it makes you feel. The more you get used to talking this way the more confident you will feel about all the challenges that come your way!

Copy

You are not supposed to copy in school; it is called cheating. And cheating in school is wrong. It is wrong because you are not doing your own work; you are stealing the work of someone else and saying it is your own. Copying in the martial arts school is a good thing, however. It is the way we learn in a martial arts school. I copied my instructor and my instructor copied their instructor. In the martial arts school you should watch the really good people and copy what they are doing. This is very different than cheating. Let's say someone in your school has really good handwriting. If you started to watch them, and began to copy them you would hold your pencil the same way and you would move it across the paper the same way. Soon you would be writing as well as they write. When you really copy someone well in the martial arts school, guess what? You're doing it well yourself.

Little Voice in Your Head

Imagine that you are lost on a trip and the only person you can ask directions from is a monkey! Would you trust a monkey to tell you the right way to go? And what if that monkey was crazy? No way would you listen to a crazy monkey! You would rather try and figure it out on your own than trust a crazy monkey. That little voice in your head that says, "I am not good enough," or "I look stupid," or "I am going to mess up," is like a crazy monkey talking in your head. When bad ideas about you creep into your head, remember it is the crazy monkey talking and he doesn't know a darn thing about anything. He doesn't know directions and he doesn't know just how good you really are.

Introduce Yourself

My first day at a new school I meet a guy named Dan. I was in the third grade and Dan came over and introduced himself. We played at recess and he introduced me to some of his friends. Dan made my first day at a good one; in fact, he made all the difference. I went home that day and without my Mom asking how things went I told her all about Dan. I felt good that I had a new friend and my mother felt good for me too. Dan made two people feel good just by being nice and introducing himself.

Remember your first day in martial arts class and how edgy you felt? Wouldn't it have been nice if some kid your age came over, asked you what your name was and told you theirs, plus shook your hand? It would have made you feel a lot better. Try this: the next time a new kid comes to the school, why don't you be the first to walk over, hold out your hand to shake and say, "Hi, my name is (put your name in here), what's yours? When they answer you say, "Nice to meet you." It is really just good manners. When people feel comfortable it makes a big difference in how well they do in class, and we want everybody to do well, right? That story about Dan from my first day at a new school? That was almost forty years ago and I still remember him to this day. That is how special it is to be welcomed and made to feel like you are one of the crowd.

Sleep

Have you ever noticed that you really like your bed, and your pillow? Have you ever noticed that sometimes you just want to lie in bed, or roll over and go back to sleep? That is because you didn't get enough sleep. When your parents tell you to go to bed and you want to stay up longer they are not doing it because they are being mean; they know that you need your sleep.

Sleep is very important for the martial artist as well as for kids. As a kid practicing the martial arts, then, sleep is twice as important! Did you know you do most of your growing while you sleep? It is true! Have you ever not gotten enough sleep? Not getting enough sleep makes you tired and you have a difficult time learning, at school and at the martial arts school. So not only is sleep important to you because you grow at night, but it is important because good sleep keeps your brain sharp and ready to learn. Try this: the next time you are asked to go to bed, don't complain, fight and throw a fit, just do it. When you get up in the morning, see how you feel. Are you rested? Do you wake up fast? Are you grumpy? Test it and see; you will be surprised by the results.

Repetition

Think back to when you first started to learn how to brush your teeth. It took a while getting the toothpaste on the brush and making sure you brushed all of your teeth, not just the ones in the front. Repetition, which means doing something over and over, was the key to getting it right. Martial arts are the same. Doing a movement over and over makes the technique, the punch or the kick second nature. Second nature means you do it without really thinking. Today when you brush your teeth notice that you don't really think about it, you just do it.

Repetition is a great way to learn things. A lot of people who play sports do this all the time. They repeat the same movement over and over again, paying attention to the littlest parts of the movement, learning how all the parts work together and how to do it the absolute best way. This repetition then gives them the skill when they need it. Think of it this way: in football a quarterback throws a touchdown pass, or a soccer goalie blocks a shot. They have done it more times in practice then they ever do it in a game. So when the game is happening they already know what it is like. So the next time you are doing drills and you think they are boring, remember it is repetition that makes you good when it counts. Oh, and when you do brush your teeth, put the cap back on the toothpaste, OK?

Before You Ask

There is an old saying that goes something like this: God gave you two ears and one mouth because you are supposed to listen twice as much as you talk. I first heard this when I was a kid and it still holds true.

Before you raise your hand to ask a question, wait and listen to the full talk the instructor is giving. When you put your arm in the air and wait to have your question answered you're thinking about the question you want to ask and not about the rest of what the instructor is talking about. Think of it this way: when your arm goes up in the air you can't listen; your brain is frozen on the question you want to ask and you aren't paying attention to anything else. Instead, wait until the instructor is done and you will find most of the time your question gets answered. If that doesn't happen and you still have a question, it will probably be a really good one! And here is a tip: if when you ask a question the instructor shares it with the whole class, then you know it was a really good one.

Too Sensitive

Sometimes you can be too hard on yourself – how bad you did in class, or how you felt left out by the instructor. Or, maybe you worry too much about getting hurt. That can be tough, but you need to firm up just a little bit. When you bring a strong mental attitude into class it helps you out in a lot of ways. You find you don't sweat the small stuff and just do the best you can, knowing some classes will go better than others. It's all a matter of knowing, and remembering, a few important things. First, the instructor would never leave you out on purpose; that is just not the way they do things. So if it happens, it is not personal; they didn't single you out to be picked on. Also, when you train in martial arts you are going to get hit, kicked and thrown to the ground; you can count on it. Usually it doesn't really hurt because of the padding and the *dojo* rules that keep people from doing dangerous things. Most of the time you just wind up being shocked at the speed or surprise of the punch or the kick. That can happen, and you know what? The more it happens the more you are going to see that it is not a big deal! Lots of kids have days when things don't go so well, and feelings will come to the surface, sometimes even tears. Another good thing to remember is that your instructor and your classmates want everyone to have a good time at the *dojo*, and that they're on your side. So try to not be too sensitive about your feelings and about taking a little punch here and there. You'll find that a little mental toughness will make your whole martial arts experience better.

Push Yourself

I once had a student that was consistently just a little behind the other kids when it was time to get up off the floor – when we finished an exercise, sit-ups, push-ups, or whatever. It didn't seem right because he worked hard; he was on time, and sometimes stayed a little after class. So I asked him, "Why is it you are always close to being last when we get up off the floor?" He said that he always tried to do one more than the number we were doing. "What?" I asked. He replied, "If the number of push-ups is twenty, I do twenty-one." He added, "I want to do more than just what is required if it makes me better." That is a good thing to remember, not just in your training but in all the things you do in life. Simply doing the minimum required is never going to get you anything other than the minimum in return. Find something where you can do a little more than just what is expected. It can be at the martial arts school, but, home and school are two other places where you can find something to do more than just the minimum. Here are a few ideas:

- Do one more of every exercise done in class.

- If emptying the dishwasher is your chore, then fill it up too.

- Look ahead at your homework; see what is next and get ahead or try extra problems that are not assigned.

- Show up at the martial arts studio early to practice.

- Be the first to line up, or be in their desk at school.

- Clear the dinner table of your plate, and everybody else's plate without being asked.

- Push the shopping cart or offer to go get some items off the grocery list.

- Or, make up your own idea!

Be Where You Are

I used to have a really tough job; I mean, one that took a lot of hours and was really difficult work. I would be at work after normal business hours and think that I should be at home, or I would be at home thinking I should be at work. It was like I was never really in the place I was supposed to be. The problem was, I wasn't as useful at work when my mind was somewhere else, and same with when I was at home. I know this sounds strange but think of it like daydreaming. Have you ever been in school and your mind kind of took you to a different place, but you never left your seat? It is the same thing, just a grown-up version. It is really important to have your mind be where your body is – keeping your mind on what you are supposed to be doing right now.

Do you think a race car driver is thinking about anything else when they are driving? What about a jet pilot? What about a steam roller driver? You can see that "being where you are" – concentrating on the thing you are supposed to do at the moment can make a big difference, or we might have a jet crash into a steam roller that runs over a race car. What does this have to do with the martial arts? Imagine if you were daydreaming or worrying about something that happened at school when you were supposed to be blocking a punch or a kick, or when your class was learning something new and important. You need to pay attention in the martial arts school and do what you're supposed to be doing to prevent somebody getting hurt and to avoid wasting everyone's time, including your own.

So if you are at the martial arts school, *be* at the martial arts school, if you are doing homework, *do* homework, eating, then *eat*. You get the picture; keep your mind and your body on what you are doing right now.

Rules Rule!

At school you get rules every day, and many of them. At the martial arts school you have many rules that you need to follow as well. While you might think that rules are there just to make life less fun, they actually make things better because they allow for big groups of people to work together. What if you just went on break from your math class whenever you wanted? What if everybody in the class did that? Your classroom would look like an ant hill, everybody coming and going and asking the same questions over and over again. It would be crazy! You would not like it and you wouldn't learn much either. The martial arts class has a lot of rules too that help your class work well together. There are rules to keep everybody from hitting each other at any time, and to learn too, but frankly kids walking around just punching and kicking randomly whenever they feel like it is kind of a funny picture. Having rules just makes sense. But an important thing to remember is that you need to just make sure you follow the rules yourself – be the leader, be the example. If you notice somebody doing something that could hurt somebody, or themselves, you can say something like, "You are going to hurt somebody; you'd better stop it." But regularly being the person that points out when others have broken the rules is kind of like being a tattletale, and that's not good. Think of rules as smart things to do to keep you safe and your life more enjoyable.

Be Your Own Leader

Some people come to class expecting to be pushed by the instructor. For example, they expect the instructor to tell them when and how to do a punch, or whether or not to try a certain move. That is all fine and good but you need to take another look at what you do in your martial arts training. You are a single person in a group of people learning your art. Because of that you need to be your own leader; you need to decide some things for yourself, things that others can't decide for you, like:

1. How hard am I going to train today? Am I going to just do enough to get by or am I going to work really hard today?

2. How much will I pay attention? Am I going to make faces in the mirror and risk being caught or am I going to keep my eyes and mind on the instructor?

3. Am I going to get to class a little early and be ready, or am I going to show up just in time and be in a rush?

4. Am I going to try something new that will be a challenge?

5. This is the question you fill in: "Am I going to _____ or just _____ ?"

Being your own leader is very important in the martial arts and even more important in your own life.

Set Time Aside for What You Really Like to Do

Let's say you really like working on a heavy bag. Kicking it is a real big deal to you; it is fun, you have a good time and you are good at it. When you find a thing you really like to do, set some time aside for that drill, form, weapon, or technique.

Make the time for what you like. And here is a trick: put it at the end of something you really have to do, something that might not be your favorite thing; it can be anything in the martial arts school or even out of the school.

Think of it this way. You finish class and ask the instructor, "May I work on the heavy bag for a few minutes before the next class starts?" and you go have at it. You could do it before class but keeping it as a reward is kind of a little trick you can use to treat yourself. You could do it this way too. You finish your homework and then you get to work on kicks in front of the mirror, or whatever it is you love to do.

Life can be full of things you don't want to do or have to do, so set time aside for what you really like to do, and save it for last, like a dessert. Remember that there is something that you are very, very at good doing. When you feel a little down about something you are *not* doing well, just remember that thing you do really well or even go do it. And finally, learning is fun. Relax and enjoy what you are doing.

Take One Thing to Your Training

"That's a lot to remember" is a phrase you might hear or even use yourself when you are learning something. Think about the first form you needed to learn in your martial arts class. That form or set most likely seemed really long, complex and difficult, but look at it now. It seems short and easy to remember now, doesn't it? Here is a way you can train smart and get better fast. Imagine that I put a giant plate of nachos in front of you and said, "Eat that." How are you going to do it? It is too big to pick up and no way can you get your mouth around it. So you pull a chip off of it, and then another, eating the plate of nachos one chip at a time until you are not hungry anymore. You can cut your martial arts training into small bites too. Just take a chip from the plate and practice one thing until it is done. Here's another thing to think about. Do you take one chip, bite half of it off, put it down, take a bite from the next piece and put it down, and then take a bite from another? No, you eat the whole piece you have in your hand before you grab another. You can help your training by doing the same thing. Take a small part of your training, work on it, and then when you are satisfied, train on something else. One chip at a time.

Be Happy

You know what? Being happy is way underrated in today's world. Being moody and dark is all cool, and that is just wrong. Being happy changes the way your body feels; you stand taller, smile, and give off happy energy. That kind of energy is what other people want to be around. Dark and moody is no fun. If you want to be dark and moody you are going to be spending a lot of time alone because nobody likes to be around that. Happy people attract other people;

just like moths go to a light bulb, people naturally want to be around happy people. Happy people also have more fun and find joy in life. Here is another thing too: being happy changes the chemistry in your brain. You learn quicker when you are happy. Try this idea: take a day and smile at people when you see each other. Make a special effort to smile in the grocery line, at school, at the table. Just try it and see what happens.

What Could I Do Better?

Sometime after class, while riding in the car on the way home, take the time to think about what you did in class. You don't need to go through the whole class, just take the first thing that comes to you and look it over in your mind.

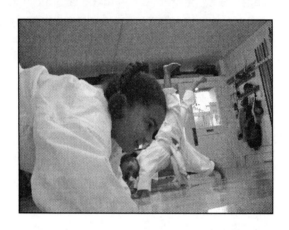

Let's just say that the first thing you think of is doing a front kick during line drills. So now ask yourself, "What would make me better next time?" It might be just lifting your knee higher by just a little bit, or putting your foot down on the ground faster. When you ask this question, think of the first thing that comes in your mind, like "kicking." Then you think of what the second thing is that you need to think about, maybe a small thing like, "Lift my knee higher." And here is what is really good about this little mental exercise of "What could I do better." The next time you do that drill in class, even though you think you have forgotten it, your mind will remember what you thought about and the idea you came up with to make yourself better and you will do it! It is like magic! But really it is just you training your mind to help your body get better. Try it! You will smile because it does work!

Don't Find Joy When Others Fail

Some people find joy when other people fail. The Germans have a big work for it, it is called *Schadenfreude.* Pronounced "shaw-den–froi-duh," it means to be happy because somebody else failed. Schadenfreude is a big, hard word for a nasty and ugly feeling. If somebody fails, you shouldn't make fun of them; that is not being nice and it makes you look really ugly while you are doing it. Instead, help them out. Think to yourself, "If that was me, what would I want somebody to do? What would make me feel better?" Here are some suggestions for what to do when this happens in your martial arts class:

1. Offer to work a little before class with them, to help fix what is wrong.

2. Suggest a training trick you use, like, "I always imagine it this way."

3. Simply say, "I had the same problem and I got over it; you will too."

4. Or something that is your own idea.

Don't find joy when others fail, it makes you a small person with a big, ugly attitude.

Matt's Rules for Life

I have great friend named Matt. Matt is easy to know and really nice. He is a big man in many ways. He played college football so he is a big, strong man. Matt has worked at the same job for twenty years and has only missed two days of work: one when his daughter was born, the other when he was sick. When it was time to paint his house he showed the neighbors the colors he was thinking of using so they could help pick it out; he didn't want to paint his house a color that might not go with the neighborhood or make his neighbors upset. Matt raised his daughter to be a fine adult, and he enjoys fishing, traveling the Western United States, and meeting new people. Matt also has what he calls "Matt's Rules of Life." They are a great set of rules that he uses, and likes to give to those kids that listen, so here they are for you to see and use too:

1. Be yourself.

2. Education? Yes!

3. Idleness is not an option.

What Matt is saying is this: First, the most important thing is to always be who you are; trust yourself, respect yourself and you will be fine. Second, go to school and do the best you can. Education makes a big difference in your life; fight for it, work for it, and don't quit. Finally, being lazy is not good; we all need to rest, but being lazy never got anybody anyplace at all.

Write "Matt's Rules of Life" on a piece of paper and put them somewhere you can see them every day – on your bulletin board in your room or on the refrigerator. Make these rules part of your life.